Look At This Woman

Look At This Woman

✦

Move Beyond the Past and the Opinion of Others to See What God Sees

Destroy the Bondage of LSE--Low Self Esteem This powerful book and the accompanying guide will show you how!

Veda A. McCoy

iUniverse, Inc.
New York Lincoln Shanghai

Look At This Woman
Move Beyond the Past and the Opinion of Others to See What God Sees

iUniverse books may be ordered through booksellers or by contacting:

iUniverse
2021 Pine Lake Road, Suite 100
Lincoln, NE 68512
www.iuniverse.com
1-800-Authors (1-800-288-4677)

ISBN-13: 978-0-595-40675-3 (pbk)
ISBN-13: 978-0-595-85039-6 (ebk)
ISBN-10: 0-595-40675-0 (pbk)
ISBN-10: 0-595-85039-1 (ebk)

Printed in the United States of America

This book is dedicated to my wonderful husband, Pastor Marvin E. McCoy. Thank you for your love, support and devotion to me. You are **the best** thing that ever happened to me. Thank you for looking at *this* woman and seeing the great things within her, long before any others could or would.

I love you dearly.

Contents

ACKNOWLEDGEMENTS

No woman is an island…and no woman accomplishes anything on her own. I have so many people to thank for this wonderful achievement. First, I want to thank my Heavenly Father, God and my Savior, Jesus Christ for the strength and ability to do this. I also want to again thank my husband, Pastor Marvin E. McCoy, for being a wonderful man and an endearing companion. To my children Myer and Johntae, I thank God for you. To my Bishop and Co-Pastor of over 17 years, Bishop Alfred A. Owens, Jr. and Co-Pastor Susie C. Owens. Thank you for the years of training, mentoring, support and opportunity. To my life-long friend and ministry colleague, Elder Vikki Johnson, thanks for the encouragement and inspiration. To my brother, Bobby Dunmore, for speaking this book into my spirit. My fellow self-published authors, Michele Irby and Gregory Cutler—thanks for listening, "prodding", and being great friends. To my fellow sisters in the ministry, to name a few, Pastor Sheretta Golladay, Elder Wasseohola Evans, Evangelist Wanda Ross, Elder Vivian Swinson, Pastor Miriam Wright, Co-Pastor Kellie Hayes, and Co-Pastor Jackie Reyes—you are THIS sister's keeper and I love you all. To the great members at Judah Christian Center, I appreciate your love, commitment and support. You are a great people to serve and to lead. I also praise God for my wonderful entire family who have always loved and supported me to the utmost. To my sisters, Precinda, Betty, and Theresa who are wonderful friends to me as well. To my mother, Irene Nicely, who took the first look and saw greatness—thank you for all you deposited into me, all that you exposed me to, all the love and guidance you gave me. And to you, the reader—thank you for taking a chance on this book. I pray it helps you to take another look and see even greater things!

Alright, let's begin!

PREFACE

Are you ready to change your life? Are you tired of being trapped by the opinions of others? Your unfortunate past or misfortunate present? Does the "view" you have of yourself prevent you from *seeing what God sees?* This book uses the story of the Luke 7 Woman—the woman with the alabaster box—to show us that it is God's opinion that matters most. Our focus should be on finding, encountering and experiencing Jesus at the various junctions of our lives. Through this process we discover our true worth and value to the world and to the Kingdom of God. Despite our past, our circumstances and even our reputations, God sees what really matters about us. I believe an encounter with God, such as the exchange that this woman had with Jesus, will show us that we should take another look at ourselves. When we have the courage to look at ourselves with complete acceptance and affirmation, others cannot help but follow our lead. Through this book, you will find redemption, restoration and hope by look at yourself through the eyes of God.

1

AN UNEXPECTED REACTION

Chapter 1
An Unexpected Reaction

A family of four went camping. Their family consisted of the mother, the father, a son and a daughter. And, as is often the case, the daughter was the apple of her daddy's eyes. To him, she could do no wrong. His chest stuck out with pride when he looked at his son. But when his eyes rested on his daughter, his heart melted and his eyes filled with tears of joy. He was so full of love for her.

During the course of the trip however, the little girl wandered off away from the camp site. The father had given strict instructions to her and her brother: They were not to go anywhere without either their mother or their father being with them. The father had warned of the dangers in the surrounding woods and how easy it was for someone to get lost. But the little girl disobeyed her father, because she was intrigued by what she imagined might be out there.

Eventually, she enters the thickest parts of the forest. The branches of the trees hid the sky and its light. Their wide trunks blocked the view of the paths. In just a short time, the little girl was completely lost and totally unable to find her way back to her family and the safety of their camp site. As time went on, the father noticed that his precious daughter was missing. He asked her mother, but she had not seen their daughter leave. He inquired of the little girl's brother, but he had been busy with his own fun. None of the other families camping near them knew anything. Panic filled the father's heart! She—his sweet, little girl—was GONE!

And so the search began. Here! There! Everywhere! The father looked for his daughter. His lost baby. Minutes turned into hours and the hours lapsed over the entire day. The day turned to evening and night was fast approaching. Time was running out and the little girl's survival was at stake. The father had to find her before she froze to death. He had to get to her before wild animals sniffed out her innocent scent and devoured her. If the father did not find his precious daughter soon, she might walk off a cliff, because the fog made it hard to see your hand in front of you. For in the woods—in the thick forest—the night is very different from the day. But of course, the little girl had no way of knowing this. If she had known, of course, she would never have gone off in the first place.

He called her name...perhaps she might hear him. He sniffed the air. Maybe he would smell her sweet scent. Realizing that she was no doubt extremely afraid, he lis-

tened for her muffled cries. He felt the air in front of him and the ground beneath him. His precious daughter might have fallen. But he heard nothing. He smelled no scent. He felt only the cold ground. Empty air. Nothing.

It seemed that all hope was lost. The little girl's disobedience would result in a tragic ending for her and heart break for this father and family. But then the father remembered! Back home the little girl had always been afraid of the dark. She simply could not stay in a room where there was no light. So, he had given her a beautiful necklace with an exquisite, heart-shaped locket. The necklace had been made especially for his little girl, and when the locket opened, a little light shine forth out of it. When he had given her this locket, the father told the little girl, "When you are afraid or if I am ever away from you, open this locket. This light represents my love for you: it shines away all of the darkness. I will never let anything happen to you." Could it be? Might the light from that locket lead the father to his precious little girl? Yes indeed! Sure enough the little girl had remembered. And it was by that little heart-shaped locket that this father found his precious little girl. When he found her, he hugged her and kissed her. He threw her up in the air and allowed her to fall securely in his strong arms. He nestled her in his chest, so that she could hear the pounding of his heart and know that she was home.

Finally, he hoisted the young girl up on his shoulders and headed back through the woods to the camp site. When they returned to the camp, everyone was still in uproar over the lost girl. By this time, the police had come and everyone's vacation had halted, so that they could look for her. Oh, the raucous she had caused! The joy she felt at being found now turned to fear. She was afraid her father would scorn her for being disobedient and causing so much trouble. It was her fault, all of this trouble. And as people turned to see that she was home, they looked at her father to see how they should respond. If he seemed angry, then they would respond in kind. But the father did none of that. He was overjoyed that his daughter who was once lost was recovered. He belted out, loud enough for all to hear, "LOOK AT MY DAUGHTER! I FOUND HER! HERE SHE IS!" And, taking their cue from him, everyone surrounded the two of them celebrating and rejoicing.

Does this story sound like you? Someone you know? Have you ever strayed away from what you knew was right, only to find yourself in need of rescue? Are you stifled by the fear that those "back home" might not understand your journey and the choices you have made?

You should know that the God, our Father, does not care what the circumstances surrounding your departure might have been. Neither does He care how long you've been gone. He is only concerned with your return. And, if you can overcome the shame and the embarrassment of what you did, then you can come to Him and find all of the love and the care you have been searching for.

What an unexpected reaction this little girl receives from her father!

I don't know about you, but I know some families where things would have happened a lot differently. After making sure the child was okay, there would have been some old fashioned whipping going on! Disobedience is one thing. But to cause uproar in the community and to bring shame upon the family is something else entirely different. But God runs His family a little differently than we sometimes do ours. Thankfully, God can see beyond the *what* and consider the *why*. God knows and He understands that we are always in need of a second chance, a second look. And God knows that He often has to speak up for us—to protect and defend us—so that others will leave us alone. By blessing us and restoring us, God allows the world to know that He is a loving father and a forgiving God.

Like the father in our story, God tells everybody, *"Look at my daughter! Look at my son!"* He lets everyone know that He doesn't care how badly we messed things up. It does not matter to God what He had to do in order to get us back home. All that matters is that we and He are connected again. What greater price could be paid than to ransom the life of Christ? What greater sacrifice could be made than the precious blood of Jesus Christ, the Son of God? But, to God, finding us is worth the expense. Our restoration is worth what God had to pay, and He is more than willing to win us back at all costs.

So do not stay away because you think you've blown it and there is no way you can recover and get back up. Pick yourself up! Don't worry about what others may think or what they may know. And, you do not have to wait for anyone to find you or to come looking for you. Jesus Christ already did that! The pathway home has been dug up, cleared and paved. All you have to do is walk on it and return to God. No long speeches or excuses will be necessary. Come home, my sister. Get up, my brother. Give it another try. Take another look. An *unexpected reaction* awaits you.

2

THE WOMAN IN THE MIRROR

Chapter 2
The Woman in The Mirror

Looking in the mirror is not always easy. Many of us rarely, if ever, look ourselves squarely in the mirror. Talking to ourselves, giving words of affirmation and reassurance, is simply out of the question. We brush our teeth while looking down, we curl our hair while carrying on conversations on the phone with friends, husbands or children. We even put on our make-up looking up at the ceiling. Phase 1 of this book's self-esteem improvement program should make looking at yourself in the mirror a part of your regular routine. You will discover that the woman in the mirror is awesome! She has a whole lot more to offer than first anticipated. Have you looked at her today? What did you say to her? What did she say to you?

Quite often the reason we do not want to look in the mirror is because we do not like what we see. In that mirror we see the hard evidence of our past. We are faced with undisputable fact that we have, as those infamous words of Ricky Ricardo would tell us, *"some explaining to do"*, for the things we've done. Certainly God does not want others to know these unfavorable things about us! Why would God want that? Doesn't He understand that where we've been and the things we've done are too embarrassing for public disclosure? *(After all we've done a whole lot worse than run away from a camp site and get lost in a forest, right?!?!?)* Those are the types of questions we begin to ask as we muster the courage to objectively look at ourselves—*the good, the bad and the ugly.* It is very easy for guilt and shame to filter in and to become a part of our self-identity. Avoiding the harsh reality of our pasts is where masks and facades come from. It is much easier to hide behind the picture that we create rather than to bare ourselves as we truly are. However, life is a multi-faceted phenomena. Today's tragedy becomes tomorrow's triumph. Yesterday's mistake paves the way for a future miracle.

In looking at the Luke 7 Woman—as she is often called—we see that her life can be viewed from multiple vantage points. What did she see when she looked in the mirror? Harlot? Perhaps. Victim? Probably. *Heroine?* Definitely not! Or, could it be? The woman, whose story is told in Luke chapter 7, is one of the most famous in scripture. Like many other women in the Bible she is an obscure character: a face and a story without a name. However, her saga is the subject of countless sermons and many songs as well.

The Bible does not tell us much about this woman, except what we find in Luke 7:37.

"And behold, a woman in the city who was a sinner, when she knew that Jesus sat at the table in the Pharisee's house, brought an alabaster flask of fragrant oil." (NKJV).

Many commentators conclude that the Luke 7 Woman was a prostitute. The Bible, however, only says that she was a "sinner". They conclude that she was probably a woman of means, because she had "fragrant oil" in an "alabaster flask", both of which were costly. Bible scholars assume that she was probably a harlot because there would have been few other ways for her to acquire the money to buy these expensive items. Also scholars understand that women who were not married or tied to their fathers' households were easy prey for victimization and discrimination because of the patriarchal, male-dominated culture of historical times. Prostitution was common among such women. Those who found themselves alone without an acceptable means of supporting themselves were often left with no other choice. Today we would certainly take issue with this generalization that a woman has to get her money from male-controlled sources or by selling her body. Simply because a modern-day woman does not have a husband or has grown too old for her father to take care of her does not mean that she must resort to becoming a woman of the night. However, during the time of the Luke 7 Woman, that is exactly the way it was. Therefore, this woman is generally referred a sinful woman, a harlot, a woman of ill-reputation.

While all of these epitaphs might be true, they might also not be accurate. I dare say that the scriptures are much more certain about another fact concerning this woman, the Luke 7 Woman. That fact is that she is indeed a **heroine**. By heroine I do not mean in the sense that she is a champion who rescues a particular group of people. Nor do I mean to imply that she goes on a murderous, revenge-filled rampage against villains or foes. Rather, I refer to the word heroine in the literary sense as being the *main character of a drama*. The Luke 7 Woman is quite a "dynamic" character and *the* key focus of a series of events leading to a glorious climax and a powerful resolution. Her life, particularly her dramatic encounter with Jesus, has a powerful message from which we can learn many things about improving our self esteem. As we read her story, we watch her metamorphosis unfold before our eyes. She goes from a bashful uninvited guest at a party where the guests thought ill of her to being the object of Jesus' attention and the subject of his lesson to Simon. Jesus says to Simon, *Simon, seest thou this woman?* In other words, Hey, Simon! Take a look at this woman and learn a thing or two!

Like the Luke 7 Woman, we are also the heroines of our own life stories. Without anyone's stamp of approval, here we are at center stage—the focus of everyone's attention. God is saying to the crowd, "Look at this woman!" And guess what? God is not hiding all the bad He knows about us. He is not ashamed of what He had to rescue us *out of*, where He had to come in order to get us out, or what He found us doing when He chose to set us free. Our past is a part of God's story. That's right. Our *history* becomes a part of **HIS STORY**, because He tells it from His own point of view. God's point of view is that we are the apple of His eye. He loves us and chooses us in spite of what we've done. When we see ourselves from God's point of view, we realize that we do not have to have anybody else's approval to be a heroine. We do not have to have a crystal clear past in order for OUR story to make an impact in the lives of others. And, perhaps most importantly, we do not have to be at the top of anybody's list of "people to know" or "people to invite", just for the blessings of God to come our way. No one wanted the Luke 7 Woman at the feast that day. No one thought she was worth an invitation. Everyone expected Jesus to shun her, to embarrass her, and to expose her. But he didn't turn her away or ridicule her. Rather, Jesus showed her off to everyone! He made her the main character—the most important person—of a story that has survived thousands of years and is still being told today.

Destiny or Just Dinner?

In Luke 7, Jesus had been invited to dinner at the house of Simon, a Pharisee. Simon's motives behind this event were undoubtedly less than pure. He was curious about this new preacher-teacher named Jesus and he wanted to see for himself what all the hype was about. But unbeknownst to Simon, while he had *coordinated* a <u>dinner</u>, God had *ordained* <u>destiny</u>!!! And God had a bigger agenda that included more than just food and fellowship. A woman, a sinner with a "reputation", shows up as an uninvited guest. She comes for one reason and for one reason only. She is there to see Jesus. And not only is she there to see Jesus, she is there to minister to Him, to bless Him. She knew she was not invited, but she went anyway. She had an extraordinary need that required supernatural attention, and she went to the one who could meet her need. She needed to see the Man who had recently begun a ministry to and for people just like her. A ministry aimed at helping the disenfranchised, the marginalized, the oppressed, the "under dog". We know from the narrative that she made her way to Jesus and began ministering to Him. If we are going to repair our damaged self-esteems and warped self-images, we must adopt the Luke 7 Woman's mentality. Get past the point of worrying about the crowd. Get past the point of what everybody knows. Face what you see in your mirror and take yourself to see Jesus!!

One might ask the question why did this woman come to the feast already prepared to minister to Jesus by washing His feet and offering Him expensive oil? I speculate that inasmuch as Simon and his guests knew who this woman was, she knew them as well. Perhaps she knew the type of person that Simon was and the type of people with whom he associated. Maybe she *knew* that if Jesus was a guest at the table of Simon, he would not be treated properly. Jesus' ministry took place in a part of the world that was extremely hot and intensely dusty. The primary modes of travel were by foot or by donkey. Much of what we read says that Jesus walked to his destinations, both near and far. Due to the intense heat and high amount of dust in the desert, hosts would often place a bowl of water at the door so that their guests could wash their feet and refresh themselves. Extremely polite and gracious guests also provided fragranced oils for the guests. And it was always the custom to greet those with whom you shared a fellowship with a holy kiss. But Simon did not do any of these things. We have already speculated as to why. Simon's motives were not to truly entertain Jesus. Simon merely wanted to see what Jesus was about. Note what Jesus says to Simon about his "hospitality".

"…I entered your house; you gave Me no water for My feet, but she washed my feet with her tears and wiped them with the hair of her head. You gave Me no kiss, but this woman has not ceased to kiss My feet since the time I came in. You did not anoint My head with oil, but this woman has anointed My feet with fragrant oil" (Luke 7:44—46) (NKJV).

The Luke 7 Woman perceived this opportunity and *seized the moment* to meet the man about whom everyone had been talking about. And, as a result she was able to change her life. Prayerfully, if everything they were saying about Him was true, He would be able to fill the void present in the depths of the Luke 7 Woman's soul. At the very prompting of a deficiency in the character of Simon, this woman lay hold of an opportunity to do something about her situation. Sometimes we must be willing to do the undesirable. After all, who wants to be identified with emulating the behavior of a harlot? Not many of us. Who wants to be compared to a woman whom no one wanted to be around? The list of volunteers is short. We must be willing to do something that we have never done before in order to get what we have never had before. This woman risked it all. She acted as a maidservant by washing the feet of Jesus. She made herself available for worship by providing a service to the Christ. She took the risk. She came into the room. She ignored the crowd. She passed by the whispers and the negative comments. She had not come to be bothered with all of those people anyway. She had come to see Jesus. And despite the fact that her life may be a little shady, we would benefit well if we would follow the Luke 7 Woman's example. A friend once told me, "Give up everything you have, so that God can give you all the things He has for you." This might mean giving up the mask behind which we have been hiding. We might have to come clean and admit that we have not always been saved. We might have to share our testimony of what God has delivered us out of and what we are *yet* believing God to set us free from. People might have to discover that although we look really wonderful on Sundays, everything in our lives is not picture-perfect. But nevertheless, we must do what we have to do. Go where we have to go! Ignore the haters! Step over the signifiers! And *get to Jesus!* Don't be afraid to look at the woman in the mirror. Don't be afraid of what she has to reveal. Jesus has considered it all and has removed the stain. Now, we must let go of the shame and come to Him. Minister to Jesus with our tears of shame, pain, disappointment and all the like. Let Him show us how to lift up our heads and hold them high. Way high!

What has been said about you? What names have you been called? Some of what people say about us is true; some of it is not. It doesn't matter. What matters is whether we are willing to take the risk, like the heroine we now call the Luke 7 Woman. As a result of her daring to do the *un*thinkable, this *un*named, *un*popular, and *un*invited Luke 7 Woman turns out to be the star of the evening! She was the heroine of the story Jesus wanted to unfold on that evening. Her life was the catalyst to a new revelation about her life—and what an *unlikely* heroine she was indeed. But that is how God works. He does not care what others see when they look at you. He only cares about His purpose for you. I say again, most of us, if we had our way, would not choose to be identified with the Luke 7 Woman. Despite the fact that we all have a past—something that God has covered and forgiven—we would shy away from saying, "Hey! I'm like that Luke 7 Woman! God worked in my life, just like He worked in hers."

And because we are so afraid of the truth and so committed to perpetuating fraud and facades, I believe that the Body of Christ is missing a major ministry opportunity. My prayer is that we will move into a dimension of ***transparency*** and that we will be able to reach out to people whose lives are not very different from the ones we came from. How many now-sober and saved alcoholics walk past a drunk to get to church each Sunday, without offering their testimony as a possible way out? How many former teenaged mothers, now married and saved, frown upon those young girls who give their bodies away looking for the same kind of love, acceptance and assurance?

We must also remember that God's purpose doesn't just pop up on the screen of your life when you come into a knowledge of Him. God's purpose has been a part of your life and of who you are since the day you were conceived in your mother's womb.

Before I formed you in the womb I knew you; Before you were born I sanctified you; I ordained you a prophet to the nations (Jeremiah 1:5).

Purpose is what got you to the point of surrender. Purpose is what helped you walk away even though you wanted to stay. Purpose helped you to put down those drugs that your body so badly craved and to throw the liquor bottle away. And purpose is continually unfolding before you. Each step of faith you take brings you closer and closer to God's *ultimate* purpose for you.

3

WHAT DO YOU SEE IN YOU?

Chapter 3
What Do You See in You?

There is a popular saying that declares, "Beauty is in the eye of the beholder." So it is with us and our lives. And, destiny, too, is in the eye of the beholder.

A two-sided rug was once on sale at a fine department store. The rug hung from the ceiling, so that people admiring it could see the intricate details on both sides of the rug. A couple wandered into the store in search of the perfect complement to their recently built home, which featured a spectacular foyer with beautiful hardwood floors. The design of the foyer called for a simple but elegant rug pattern. When they happened upon one particular rug, the wife ventured to the side of the rug where the design appeared to be quite fancy. The husband went to look at the other side where the soft colors flowed in and out of a beautiful pattern that would fit the foyer perfectly. The wife, unable to see the side with the less exuberant design, concluded that the rug was a bit too fancy for the design scheme of the couple's foyer. The husband, unable to see what his wife was looking at, did not understand her view point at all. From where he was standing, the color scheme was perfect. The soft design of the rug would perfectly accent the entrance to their home. The two argued back and forth for a few moments, until finally the wife said, "Honey, come over here so you can see what I see!"

Many of us suffer from the same problem that the couple experienced. We argue back and forth with God that what He has in mind for us just is not there. Oh we do not argue outright, but we argue with our failure to move forward to pursue and accomplish the things God tells us we each can do. For some of us, our self-view is obscured by our past. We are hindered from realizing our true worth and value by the things we have gone through that have left us seeing ourselves from a tainted point of view. Sermons that rave about how wonderful we are work very well at church or during the conference. But when it comes to putting those ideas into action and applying them to our lives, we often fail mostly because we are not able to see the value and the worth that God sees when he looks at us, His beloved. And there is so much truth in the statement, "Until *we* can see it, it will never matter that anyone else can."

Often, when we give our life to Jesus Christ, we make significant changes in our behavior, habits and language. We desperately want people to see and affirm the "newness" of our lives. We desire that they see what we believe is now within us and what the Word of God declares is indeed there. We want God's presence to be obvious and the work of His Holy Spirit to manifest powerfully to everyone who sees us. Most times, however, people's opinions of us do not change right away if ever at all. Our family members and close friends who think they know us so well are especially incapable of seeing the new us. To these people, we will always be what and who we were in the days of our past. For some, we will never be anything more than what we have always been. It is during these times when we must accept the fact that people see what they want to see. Beliefs can comprise a person's reality. No amount of arguing or pleading will change the way they see us. And unfortunately we usually learn to judge our worth and value based upon what other people see in us. As children, we look to our parents or caregivers to give us signals that we mattered in this world. As infants, whether we know it or not, we instinctively seek to make these people smile. When we see joy in their eyes resulting from something "cute" we have done, we learn to repeat the behavior again and again just to see them smile at us. We soon learn that our job as infants is to figure out what will make these silly grown ups smile! Being smiled at sure does make a person feel warm, loved and appreciated. It is not until later that we realize you will never please all of the people all of the time. It is not until later that we realize you must love yourself first. It is not until later that we gain the knowledge that it will not matter at all what others see in us, if we do not already see greatness in ourselves. It is not until later that we learn that only in pleasing God can you find the peace, joy and happiness that our souls seek. And for most of us later includes many failed attempts at getting validation from outside sources. We try and try again to get others to *see* us for who we are. And in seeing us, we hope they will love us. We hope that in their eyes we will see the sparkle that tells us we are indeed beautiful, despite our flaws and shortcomings.

However, the great news is that God's view of us is not dependent upon what others see or do not see in us. God does not make declarations about our lives based upon what people may think. People's views are limited by their *beliefs.* God sees us based upon what *He knows!* Furthermore, God has a way of revealing things to people and making His plans for your life plain to those around you. And, when He does, there is no mistaking the revelation. For example, when Jesus interacted with the Luke 7 Woman, He saw something in her that the others around her just flat out rejected.

"If he were indeed a prophet, he would know what kind of woman it was who was touching him." (Luke 7:39)

That was their initial reaction—the men, the Pharisees, the traditional Jews—to look at where the woman was, where she had come from and what she was perhaps involved in. Her gender, her social class, her economic status were all blinders to the "potential" that Jesus saw in her. Her worth as a servant and a worshipper, however, out-shined all of the negative and it caused Jesus to silence the nay-sayers. Jesus saw that she brought her very best to offer to Him in praise. She brought her fragranced oil inside of her alabaster box. She poured out her best at the feet of Jesus. She bowed down at the feet of Jesus and gave the very best she had to give. All that she had she offered at Jesus' feet. She did not bother to ask the onlookers what they were staring at or whom they were talking about. She did not even allow the ghosts and skeletons from her past, still vivid in her mind, to stop her. To her the only thing that mattered is what she could see in the eyes of Jesus. She saw hope, she saw possibility, she saw that maybe for once, she would not have to prove her worth by how well she looked or to whom she was connected. She made a great sacrifice of praise pouring the oil on the feet of Jesus. She felt her passionate praise so deeply, that scripture tells us she began to wash His feet with her tears. This was no performance. Her acts were not of someone who merely wanted to be seen with the latest, most popular preacher. She cried tears of praise at the feet of our Lord, Jesus Christ. Others around might have asked, *"Why is she crying? Who has harmed her?"* Perhaps in the past she had cried because she was alone. Maybe she had cried because she was jilted by a lover. Perhaps the privileged women of the town had shunned her once again, and so she had cried. But this time, these were not the causes of her tears!! This time, she cried because the eyes of Jesus held no prejudice against her. These tears were tears of love, gratitude, and worship. Jesus' eyes pronounced no judgment, no condemnation. Rather, these eyes reflected redemption and salvation. And regardless of what she might see in the eyes of everyone else, Jesus' eyes told her all that she ever longed and needed to hear. The eyes of Jesus said to her, *"I see YOU. I SEE you. I acknowledge your sacrifice and its great cost. I accept and receive your worship. You are at last at home in my love. You will never, ever have to leave again."*

Are these not the things we long to hear? The unconditional love we long to feel? The uninhibited worship we desire to give? If you're like me, the answer to each of these is yes. Yes! Yes! Yes! And it is hard to believe that it starts with what we see in and believe about ourselves. But it does. So, for the believer who wants to move beyond her past and the opinions of others, the image of her beauty must be seen through the eyes of the most important beholder of all. God. Stop worrying about what people *see* when they look at you. Leave the change in what people may or may not see to God. Look to God for validation and confirmation, and move forward with what you *see* through *His* eyes. God will see things in us that we cannot see; nevertheless, we must trust that God's vision is the real deal. Likewise, God will see things in us that others just simply cannot fathom. We must accept the fact that when others do not know what God knows, and they often cannot see what God sees. And so when God says there is value, purpose and destiny in us, people's response may be, ***"Who are you looking? HER!?!? I don't see that at all!"*** But have faith. Keep moving forward. Don't sweat it! Or, as the Word of God says, *"Let not your heart be trouble. Neither let it be afraid."* Ask God to help you put on a pair of *God glasses* that you may be able to see yourself from *His* point of view. Do not allow what others *choose to see* or what they *refuse to see* stop you from having an encounter with God

At it was with our sister, the Luke 7 Woman, so let it be with you and me. We must be so convinced that *God knows!* We must so trust what *God sees!* We must not waver when we come out of our private, intimate worship sessions. What we think we saw, we did indeed see. Our eyes were not playing tricks with us. Our minds were not deceiving us. There is purpose in us. There is destiny all around us. A bright and meaningful future awaits us. When we start going back to school, writing business plans, spending more time with our families and children, exercising again and all the things we dream of doing, many will not understand. They may look at us strange as if we've lost our minds. We will then have a right to ask them, *What are YOU looking at? What's wrong with YOUR vision?!? Can't you see what I see?* Perhaps they are still looking through the eyes of judgment and self-righteousness. Maybe they are still wearing the Simon-glasses or Pharisee-goggles. But we cannot concern ourselves with what others cannot see in us. We cannot delay moving forward because of what they *still* see. Our concern is only what Christ sees.

What do YOU see in You?

4

TURNING HEADS:
OUR TURN ~ OUR TIME

Chapter 4
Turning Heads ~ Our Turn, Our Time

Hey, Simon! Take a Look at This!

In the previous chapter we talked about facing the truth about ourselves. We discussed being certain that God's view of us is good, and that we should form our self-image from *this* particular picture. However, I am aware that simply saying your past does not matter and actually walking in the victory of that reality are two completely different things. You might say, *"You just don't know the things I have done!"* Many of us feel that the preachers and worship leaders who exhort us to forget about our past mistakes and forge forward as if nothing else matters just do not understand where we have been and what we have gone through. It occurs to us that such rhetoric sounds great in church and may perhaps work for others. But it simply does not apply to us. We are different, because we've done so many disparaging things. We need *a lot* of God's forgiveness.

To make matters worse, it often seems that no matter how we try to get away from our past, the past will not free us from its grips. It simply will not allow us to escape. Our past looms around us, constantly impacting our *now* moments. The past impacts us even when we are unaware that it is doing so. We've been rejected in the past, so we push people away to safeguard ourselves from being rejected again. We stumbled out of an abusive relationship, so our defense mechanisms now warn us that everybody else is an abuser as well. Our mothers did not give us affection, so we run here and there looking for the love we craved from her. No matter how hard we cry at the altar, run around the church, and slap our neighbor high-five, our present-day neediness and co-dependency make it difficult for us to see ourselves in a new light and to continually walk in this new existence. We often feel that life will not get better; things will remain the same. It seems the world is against us, and we are forever doomed to repeat self-destructive cycles. We will never fully realize the joy and peace that the Christian life promises. The preacher is talking about somebody else. Not me. Or is she? Consider this story.

A Christian woman wanted to get married for several years. She faithfully waited and refused to compromise. Finally, her knight-in-shining armor arrives and relentlessly pursues this waiting woman. The prince says and does all the right things to gain her affection. Once she's smitten, the two marry. However, like so many couples, the honeymoon period doesn't last very long. She immediately finds out things about her spouse that, had she known about them before, might have prevented her from saying "I do." Whatever his shortcomings may have been, it really does not matter. Poor money management, filthy house keeping habits, obnoxious snoring at night all qualify as quick honeymoon-enders and lead to those ever-famous words: *If I had only known.* Some knights never soil their shining armor with poor housekeeping habits or personality flaws. Rather, they make the painfully heartbreaking mistakes that include adultery, infidelity, lying, and the like. Still, the once-bedazzled wife is left with a reality much different than the one she dreamed of and anticipated. Sound familiar? If not you, then *maybe somebody you know.*

If this knight-in-shining armor allows his faults and deficiencies to discourage him, he might give up on the relationship and say there is no use in trying. This prince might wrongfully conclude that his bride will never forgive him. However the knight-in-shining armor takes a risk and responds differently. This knight-in-shining armor realizes that his cover is blown, but he does not give up. Instead, he begins to apologize to his now-wise wife. He treats his bride with extra care and kindness. Realizing that there is nothing he can do about his recent blunders or the imperfections in his personality, the knight-in-shining armor finds other ways to shine. He thanks his bride for being so understanding and forgiving. The more she forgives, the more he thanks. The more he thanks, the more she is inclined to overlook a few things here and there. Eventually, the shock of what it means to actually live with someone day in and day out—the good, the bad and the ugly—wears off. And a little bit of the fantasy returns. The wife is able to focus on other, more positive qualities about her husband. He is, after all, so cute when he begs. He can sure fry some chicken. The husband's praise and the buttering up allow this wife to take another look and to remember the treasure she once saw in her husband.

When we have true worship encounters with God, the exact same thing can happen to us. We are able to turn our focus away from the things that hold us back and take another look at ourselves. As we have previously stated, when we see ourselves differently others will follow our lead. It becomes our time to turn a few heads. The greatness within us and the bright future ahead of us become the objects of attention, not the past behind us. What lies ahead of us beams so brightly that it outshines any attempt to bring up what we may have done, gone through or experienced as indictments against us. Like Jesus told Simon, *"Hey,*

Simon! Take a look at this woman." In essence, Jesus was saying take another look at somebody you have overlooked before. Take another look at the woman you have looked down on before. She who was shunned and ignored is now turning heads and glorifying God.

Our transformations are the same as that of the Luke 7 Woman. You will begin to run into people who have not seen you in a while, and they will automatically recognize the change in you. Your response to situations and circumstances—so drastically different from the way you responded in the past—will cause people to turn their heads in your direction and ask, *"What's up with her?"* My sister, it is now your time and your turn to cause some minds to wonder and some heads to turn. Yes, time to stop hiding behind your fears and your old beliefs. *It's head turning time!*

Another thing we must understand is that God went even further than simply turning our past around. In addition to forgiving us as if our past never happened, we can rejoice at the fact God knew all about our past before any of it happened, and He did not care. He loved you anyway. God, in His omniscient knowledge, foreknew and foresaw your mistakes, misjudgments, miscalculations, and the like. And it did not matter to Him and it did not alter the future He planned for just you. He died for you anyway. He purposed you for greatness *anyway!* Look at our heroine, the Luke 7 Woman. Certainly her reputation was not hidden. The Bible refers to her as *a woman in the city* (Luke 7:37). And later, Simone questioned Jesus' validity as a prophet, because if [he] knew what type of woman" it was who was bestowing favors upon him, Jesus would want no part of it. But Jesus *did* know. When He commanded Simon to look at *this woman* He was not asking Simon to turn away from her past and ignore it. The woman's past was a large part of her appeal. The fact that she did not let her past hinder her from offering true worship and service to The Christ, was, in my opinion, one of the reasons Jesus took special note of her. She needed a lot of His love, forgiveness, compassion and mercy. But she worshipped *anyway*. We need to adopt this *anyway* mentality that worked so well for the Luke 7 Woman—and for Jesus! Push forward *anyway!* Pursue your destiny *anyway!* Ignore what people may think or say and change your view of yourself *anyway!*

Our heroine, the Luke 7 Woman, had many things that she had done wrong. She was out of step, out of place, out of line, and out of options. So, when she found unconditional love and acceptance in the eyes of Jesus, she felt utterly grateful.

Her gratitude was apparent in her actions. As a result, she became the poster girl for how you show appreciation and love. Her past was not a hindrance, it was the basis of her promotion.

So, my friend, move forward to your destiny. Pursue your dream. Conquer your fears. Because there is nothing that you have done—nothing from which you are running—that will shock God. He knows and *He does not care.* He chooses you anyway. He saves you anyway. He delivers you anyway. He calls, anoints, appoints, and sends you anyway.

The time has passed for being ashamed of your past, for being ashamed of what God has done in your life and where He has brought you from. Some people say that God wipes away the past and does not remember it. To a certain extent, this is true. However, there is nothing hidden from God. On the contrary, He sees the past but chooses to ignore it, because His love for us far exceeds any depth of sin and shame we can sink to.

Like the young girl in our story, our mistakes and wanderings do not matter to God, our Father. He searches for us, until He finds us. We are on His heart and His mind. God sees the part of us that matters most. God sees us for who we really are. He sees the testimony of victory made possible only by our past. He sees the complete devotion we have for the *debtor* who forgave us for much and set us free from many things. Like the two debtors in John 7:41 and 42, it is the one who is absolved of the most debt who loves the most. God sees beneath the hard shell that life often forces us to create, and He peers beyond the sad eyes that shame and embarrassment turn toward the ground. God sees a heart filled with love and gratitude that is turned *solely* towards Him. And, it is this type of devotion that qualifies us for *head turning time!*

5

SEEING ALL OF YOU

Chapter 5
Seeing All Of You

Let's go a little deeper. Although when we realize that the Luke 7 Woman has something to offer—regardless of her background—it makes us wonder just what it was. Of course, we can always count on Jesus Christ to see the best in everyone. But what is it exactly that Jesus saw in this woman we've been reading about? How is it that a woman whose background was at least questionable causes Jesus to make Simon and the others take another look? No one would question that her lifestyle would cause people to look at her. However, the reason for looking comes into question. Why bother? What could a reformed prostitute (if indeed that is what she was) have to offer us? What in the world could she possible teach us?

Certainly this was the mentality of those who had gathered at Simon's house. When Jesus asked the question, *"Seest thou this woman?"* surely Simon and the other guests' immediate response was, "Yes! We see her!! So what?" Surely they had seen her before and perhaps had even shared a few intimate moments with her! But they probably did not expect for Jesus to make an ***example*** of her. And—being pious and religiously correct—they certainly did not need for this woman to teach them anything about worship, spirituality or godly living. If anything, they expected Jesus to look down on her, to belittle her, to embarrass her—as *they* would have done. But Jesus did none of these things. Jesus wanted them to see something else in our heroine, this Luke 7 Woman. He had another opinion, and he felt differently about what the guests could learn from the Luke 7 Woman.

We should be grateful for this exchange and the outcome. Why? Because Jesus' attitude towards her gives us hope as well. I'm sure we could look at our pasts and our backgrounds and conclude that there is nothing special or noteworthy about them. We might even conclude that we should hide under a rock. Some might opine that we would be the last to show our faces to the world and do public ministry. Unlike the Luke 7 Woman, if we were in a public setting like this dinner at Simon's house, we might feel more inclined to blend in with the background. Maybe we would be afraid that if others were to truly see us, they would see what ***we've*** always seen. Failure. Disappointment. Mistakes. Hopelessness. Embarrassment. Shame. Need I say more?

To take this a step further, we can also say that by calling attention to the Luke 7 Woman, Jesus was in a sense drawing the attention away from Simon and the other snooty guests. They viewed themselves as the ones who had it *going on*. They knew what the law required and what it meant to walk in ways they thought pleased God. But the One who really mattered didn't think so! When Jesus was looking for an example of someone who truly knew how to worship and how to "show the love", He didn't call attention to any of the *likely ones*. He commanded them to reconsider, to reevalute, to reexamine the person they considered to be the worst of the lot. That's right! Our friend: the Luke 7 Woman.

So, in light of these facts we can walk in hope. Our hope rests in the fact that God always finds a way to use what everyone else says is useless. He always offers chances to those whom others turn away. The good news of the gospel is that there is nothing in our lives that is so bad or so sinful that the love of God cannot find us in it and rescue us from it. The truth of the matter is many people give up on us too soon. They walk away before the final word is given. They leave the movie before the credits roll up. They exit right before the final curtain. But Jesus, our Savior, is not like everybody else. He saw something in the Luke 7 Woman and He sees something in us. Our job is to figure out what. What is it that Jesus sees? Why does He refuse to give up on us? Why won't Christ just let us go in peace? Go back to our former lives. We were more comfortable there anyway. Like the saying goes, *it is better to deal with the devils you know than to face the ones you do not know*. But Jesus is always sending signals to us that *it is not over for us!* That encouraging phone call. That heart-moving song. The unexpected card in the mail. These are all ways that Jesus says, *"Take another look. Don't give up yet. There's more to you than you think. You are not done yet. Your life is not over. There is still something in your life worth looking at."* You ask what it could be. I say that once again our heroine tells us. The story of the Luke 7 Woman also reveals what it is we have to offer. What Jesus saw in her, he looks for in us. If we want to be true worshippers, there is a pattern to follow. Jesus' purpose in this story was to show us the way, the more excellent way. And, in this instance, He did exactly that.

Change Your Self View

I cannot stress to you enough the importance of shedding the view of others and replacing it with what Jesus sees when He looks at you. In addition to her *past*, Jesus also saw her *posture,* her *praise* and her *possibility*. All of that, you might ask? Yes, indeed, all of that! And my wonderful sister, our future holds the same promise, the same hope. Once again, let's turn to our heroine to see if she can help us *change our view*.

Her Past

When Jesus told Simon to look at this woman, Jesus was very much aware of the fact that Simon would remember that the woman had "a past." Simon knew that the woman had a reputation for a certain way of life. However, because Jesus is the Great Emancipator, He does not need to shy away from questionable reputations. I am not sure whether the woman knew that Jesus was using her as an example or not, but it really does not matter. How often are we being examined by people, considered by the crowed, evaluated by the audience and we do not know it? Let God worry about what others are saying about your past. Stop running away from your calling and your destiny, because you are afraid that someone might remember when. Do not suppress your gifts any longer, for fear that you might be found out. If God is pushing you to the frontline, run to your future with full speed. Refuse to be stopped or held back any longer. Put your past in the hands of God, your Rescuer and your Redeemer. He sees and knows everything. And if God doesn't think you have anything to hide then why should you? If God doesn't think that you are too dirty, too shameful, too filthy to be used for His glory, then do not get in your own way.

This does not mean that you go around bragging about your past. Nor does it mean that you cannot feel sorry for the wrong that you have done. The point is to *see* your past. See the lessons it taught you. See the pain it caused you. See the blessing it can be to someone else who is trapped in a similar situation. The experience you acquired in your past can be tools of ministry to help someone else. But it takes the wisdom of God and the power of the Holy Spirit to make it happen. We must remember that our lives are now hid in the life of Jesus Christ. His agenda is the only agenda that matters. And, when the time is right, He will raise you up and allow you to minister through your experience, from your experience and in spite of your experience. The difference between doing this under God's power rather than doing it in our fleshly pride is that we can **minister from our without ministering our experience**. Your past is the fuel and the power that keeps the engine of your ministry going. But you can use that power without anyone ever having to know the details of where it came from or how you got it. If and when the time comes for you to share your testimony, God will open up the appropriate door and create a suitable platform. Many of us are wives, mothers and leaders in our communities and churches. No one is an island and no woman stands alone. So, we must consider that our past—and the revealing of our past—will impact lives besides our own. Most of us have been delivered from situations and experiences that need explanation and clarification. Just putting it out there, even in the name of "ministry", without the anointing of God and according to His divine purpose does not glorify God. And often we end up making ourselves look important and impressive for a few minutes, but doing more damage to the purpose of God in the long run.

Am I contradicting myself? I do not think so. We should be proud of the fact that we are still here. We should glorify God that we are delivered. And we should not allow anyone to make us feel common or unclean because we have a past. *Everyone has a past!* But at the same time, we must realize that it is in Jesus Christ that we live, move, and have our being. Our lives are now lived for His glory alone. And our experiences are included in that as well. The Bible says that the steps of a good woman are ordered by the Lord. Let God order all of your steps, including the steps of using your past to show the devil that it is God who is all powerful, and He is in control. God did not deliver you and get you out for you to remain in the shadows. You are a tool—a weapon in the arsenal of God—who will be used to bring the kingdom of darkness down. Your past and your victory over it will be used to help someone else be set free and delivered.

Just like our heroine, the Luke 7 Woman, we have a past. And when God brings us to the forefront and is ready to use us for His glory, He will tell the world, *"Look at this Woman!"* At that point, our pasts will not be able to stand up against the power of God that has been produced in us.

Her Posture

In this Bible narrative, we see that the Luke 7 Woman came into the party uninvited. She did what she had to do. Sister-Girl needed to see Jesus, and she did not let the fact that she was not on the VIP list stop her. But notice that she did not barge into the room and start yelling and screaming, making demands about what she wanted and needed. Rather, she assumed a certain posture: the *posture of a servant.* A true worshipper is one who *waits on God* with the attitude of a servant. As we mentioned earlier, she noticed that no one was ministering to certain needs of Jesus, so she seized the moment and took her destiny into her own hands. Our heroine was as smart as she was humble. And to her credit, Jesus took notice. I firmly believe that Jesus was making a striking comparison to the difference between the treatment he received from Simon, the so-called host, and this

Luke 7 Woman—an *uninvited* guest. He took note of her posture, and I believe he wanted Simon to notice it as well.

The tradition during this historic time was that people ate on tables that were very close to the floor. Sometimes they sat on the floor, but often they stretched out in front of the tables and propped themselves up on their elbows to access the contents of the table. Sometimes, people stretched their feet out in front of them. They might not have paid particular attention to what was going on in the area of their feet. The Luke 7 Woman bowed herself at the feet of Jesus, and she began to wash his feet. Perhaps even she positioned herself slightly behind His feet, so that she would not draw Jesus' attention away from His conversation. Her objective was to *serve Him.* Therefore, she chose the posture of humility and servitude. Then, she washed His feet with the water and with her tears. She sought His feet to serve Him, not His hands to get something from Him. She humbled herself to the position of a servant, rather than trying to get in Jesus' face to impress him. But the Luke 7 Woman did not let her posture of servitude cause her to put on false humility. Often we are not sure how to mesh the two together—*1.* humility in the presence of God and *2.* hunger for the things of God. We fear that others will misunderstand our desperation and mistake it for disrespect and gall. But this woman—the Luke 7 Woman—had the right posture, and she went forward with what was on her heart to do. She served Jesus at His feet. And as she fulfilled that mandate, her obedience propelled her to a higher position. She started with humility, but she ended with greatness. The result was that she got what she needed. I believe this is what most of us seek. The simple process of going after what we truly want and actually receiving it.

My sisters, we will do well to learn from our heroine's actions. Many times, we are frustrated and hurt by what we've been through. We end up with a chip on our shoulder. We begin to feel as if we are owed something, even if only an apology. We have been cheated out of many basic necessities of personal development, such as nurturing, reassurance and opportunity. These simple necessities of existence were often not available to many of us. Those who were supposed to protect us did not do so. The people who should have been there for us were nowhere to be found. And the results are barriers and attitudes. We fortify ourselves against being hurt again. And many times, the *posture* that we take keeps us from being in the right *position* to receive our blessing. We fear humbling ourselves to God, because He too might fail or disappoint us. We certainly are not interested in humbling ourselves before a man or a woman—be it a leader, a sister-friend, or even a companion. But, remember our heroine. She took the risk and gained much from it. I challenge each of us to follow suit. Throw off the baggage from your past. Drop the load you have been carrying, and get down on your knees in the presence of the One who can make a difference. You do not have to stand guard over your heart anymore. This area is safe. In the presence of the Holy One there is fullness of joy! Release yourself from fear-induced inhibitions and launch out into the deep. Plunge into your future and grab hold of your destiny.

Her Praise

When it truly mattered, this woman found something to give the Savior. Again, most people would look at her and think that she did not have anything worthwhile to offer. People look at us and think the same thing. They ponder what could we possibly have to say that would encourage anyone? Our past circumstances and our current predicaments make onlookers doubt that we are of any value at all. But there is something we have to offer. This Luke 7 Woman probably had to put on a different thinking cap. If indeed she was a woman of the night she was accustomed to offering her body and her affection to get what she wanted. However, this time things were different. She no doubt had heard how the Savior was a *different kind of man,* and she could not come to Him with the same strategy and antics. So she went within her precious treasures and brought Him costly, fragranced oil. This precious oil was placed in an equally costly box made of alabaster. Can you see the miracle? Is it *now* clear why our heroine was worth looking at? Do you know why *you* need to step out of the shadows into the light of possibility? There is something inside of us that God desires. And, when we offer it from the place of brokenness and despair, it becomes even more rich and valuable to God. That thing, my sister, is our pure, uninhibited praise. Birthed out of our joy and our pain, our praise glorifies God and brings the right kind of attention to us. The attention that says it is not about us, but it is about what God has done in us. The Luke 7 Woman brought her costly oil and put it in an expensive box. She broke the box in order to pour the oil out. The best praise is produced from broken vessels. There is nothing that God appreciates more than our willingness to bring our brokenness to Him and offer even that to Him in the form of praise. This is exactly what our Luke 7 Woman did. She worshipped, she praised, she extolled, she bowed herself down. She gave Jesus the best she had to offer, regardless of the personal cost to her. Personally, I am impressed. She was a woman of means, she was a woman who could save, *and* she was a woman who knew when it was time to cash in on an investment! What better place to sow the see such a seed of sacrifice than at the feet of Jesus.

Do you think you are all out of options? Have you nothing else to give? Do not count yourself out just yet! Within your heart and soul is an earnest praise that will move the heart of God. That place of utter dependence, total devotion, and relentless pursuit is the point from which we offer the sweet praises unto God that only we can give.

Jesus took note of the Luke 7 Woman's praise because it was pure—especially in contrast to the superficial attention the hosts and other guests were giving Him. And we must remember that what we offer God does not have to be *perfect*, it need only be **_pure!_** And the same way that Jesus took note of her praise, He will also gladly receive ours as well.

Her Possibility

If you only see what you've always seen, then you will only be what you've always been!

You have to be able to *see* the potential in you. You must visualize yourself as someone who can be better—more productive, happier, more fulfilled. It is such a comforting reality to know that when God looks at us the first time, He sees what we can be *after* our *divine makeover*. He sees it in us right at that very moment. And God is not deterred by the process that must take place in order for our potential to explode into our present and create for us a new reality. God saw great potential in our Luke 7 Woman, even in her present, unfavorable condition. She had the potential to be an example. She had the possibility to be a worshipper. She had the possibility to show that none of us is better than the rest of us. She had the potential to dispel a few myths about women. She had potential and possibility in ways she had never imagined. To her, the quest to see Jesus was motivated by pure desperation. However, she got so much more out of the deal. Her life was forever changed. Jesus finally says to this woman, *"Your faith has saved you. Go in peace." (Luke 7:50).* Can you imagine the amazement of all the nay-sayers who were standing around??? Surely God could not save a woman like *this* woman! And what did it matter whether *she* had peace or not?? Sounds like some women I know, women whom people have written off, put in a box, categorized, disenfranchised. Sounds like *me!* Sounds like *you!* And I submit to you that God desires to cause the same kind of impact in our lives. I have long tired of church as usual. I am convinced that we need our lives, our hearts, our minds, and our outlooks to be *divinely changed*, when we come from a worship experience. Because there is potential locked up inside of us that has been held hostage by the events of our pasts, our socioeconomic status, the opinion of others, our gender, our skin color, our complexion, our hair texture, and the list goes on and on. And it is through meeting Jesus and desperately pursuing him that our potential is unlocked—*forever*—and freed to produce for the Kingdom of God.

APPENDIX

✦

The Journey to Wholeness

Five Helpful Stages to an Improved Self-Esteem and a Healthier Self-Image

Stage 1
Getting Started

Stage 1—Getting Started

How do we correct a self-image that has been broken for so long? How do we change the way we see ourselves? It is true that what you see in you is what matters most. The Word of God tells us that we are fearfully and wonderfully made. However, many of us do not grow up with this kind of teaching and reinforcement present in our lives. But once you realize your true value, you must allow the revised reality it to reshape your self-image. Build your image of yourself around what you know to be God's image of you. Determine your self value based on the sacrifice Christ made for you, because He deemed you to be ***worth the price!***

The first stage on this journey consists of two parts: an anointed prayer with three powerful affirmations and an exercise of self-celebration. Copy the prayer on a note card and place it on your dresser or vanity mirror. As you continue with your reading over the next few days, go back and repeat the prayer and affirmations at the start of your day. The prayer can be prayed while you lay in bed, preparing to meet the day. Or, it can be said before you retire in the evening. Try to recite the affirmations while looking in the mirror.

Prayer

Dear God,

*I am here because you created me, and I have value because I come from you
and I belong to you.
Help me to see those things when I look at myself today.
In Jesus Name,
Amen.*

Affirmations: (Remember to repeat our mantra—*"Look At This Woman…"*)

I am HAPPY to be ALIVE!

I am GOOD just because I am God's Daughter!

My life is GOOD because God is in it!

Memorize this prayer and these affirmations, so that when the old tapes of self-doubt, low self-esteem and other people's opinions plague your mind, you can

counter them with these new, positive thoughts. At the end of the each day, celebrate yourself by doing something just for you. It could be giving yourself just
one flower or even a smile at yourself in the mirror. Whatever it is, whether large
or small, take the time each day to celebrate your new vision of yourself. Record
your self-celebrations on the next few pages or in your journal.

Stage 1 (Part II)—   *Journal Of Self Celebrations*

Day 1 _____

Today, I celebrated myself by _____
_____

Day 2 _____

Today, I celebrated myself by _____
_____

Day 3 _____

Today, I celebrated myself by _____
_____

Day 4 _____

Today, I celebrated myself by _____
_____

Day 5 _____

Today, I celebrated myself by _____
_____

Day 6 _____

Today, I celebrated myself by _____
_____

Day 7 _____

Today, I celebrated myself by _____
_____

Stage 2

Continuing the Process

Stage #2—Continuing the Process

Before you begin Stage 2 of this process, take a few minutes to reflect on the activities from Stage 1. Respond to these questions.

How did it feel to celebrate yourself EVERYDAY? _____
_____

What did you learn new about yourself in the process? _____
_____

How did the activity change your view of yourself? _____
_____

Now you are ready to continue on with the activities in Stage 2.

What do you see when you look at your life? Who looks back at you when you look at the woman in the mirror? Are you ashamed of her? Do you love her in spite of herself? Do you only see the negative? The mistakes? The failures? The disappointments? The foolish folly of her youth? Look again…God sees something else entirely different. God sees all of the pieces coming together to a nice picture. A beautiful picture indeed.

For the next seven days, say the following prayer and affirmations each morning. At the end of each day, complete the chart on the next page. This time, for the prayer try kneeling beside your bed or chair. Continue to repeat the affirmations while look in the mirror.

Prayer:

Dear God,
I thank you for the courage to face myself in the mirror. I thank you for taking all of me and all of my story and for loving me unconditionally. Help me to do the same.
In Jesus Name,
Amen

Affirmations: *(Remember to Repeat the Mantra—"Look At This Woman...")*

I Believe What God Says About Me!
I Believe in Myself More Than I Believe In Anyone Else!
I Believe in ALL my Dreams!

Stage 2—The Journey Continues   *Journal for Self-Reflection*

Day	Today, as I looked in the mirror, I felt *(Try to use feeling words, such as awkward, embarrassed, warm, proud, etc.)*	Compared to yesterday, today I felt *(Worse, Same, Better)*
Day 8		
Day 9		
Day 10		
Day 11		
Day 12		
Day 13		
Day 14		

Stage 3

Seeing IS Believing

Stage 3—Seeing Is Believing

This exercise is powerful! Try it with a friend or prayer partner. It is also excellent for a woman's group. Each woman will need a small, hand-size mirror. Hold your mirror up in front of your friend and ask her, *"What do you see in this mirror?"* Write down your friend's responses about what she sees in her mirrored reflection. Encourage her to be honest. Next, tell your friend what you see when you look at her. Be honest and share what you truly see. Ask your friend to write down your responses on a separate sheet of paper. Compare your friend's list with the one you recorded of her responses. How are they the same? Different?

Now, trade places and give the mirror to your friend to hold up in front of you. Your friend will repeat our mantra to you *"Look at This Woman"*. Ask yourself, *"What do I see in this mirror?"* Next, your friend will share what she sees when she looks at you. Then, you will write down what she says and compare your list with the one your friend recorded with your responses. Keep in mind that it is often easy to see the good in someone else, but it is hard to see our own positive traits. Record your thoughts in a journal or place of safekeeping.

Affirmations:

> *In the Eyes of God, everything in my life is perfect because He can see what He' working out in me*

> *I can do all things through Christ who strengthens me and lives inside of me.*

> *God has given me the power to speak my life into existence. I will speak great and mighty things over me and my life.*

> *I BELIEVE that I will HAVE whatsoever I say.*

Stage 4

Freedom Through Forgiveness

Stage 4—Freedom Through Forgiveness

The power of forgiveness can set you free from years of emotional and mental bondage. Often, we are prevented from seeing our true selves because we are locked in the constant rewinds and replays of painful memories from our past. I have seen this strategy in many forms, such as the "burn books" many therapists recommend. However, in this stage you will do more than merely write a letter describing an offense or hurtful situation from your past. Although you will most likely not mail these letters, **burning them might not be a bad idea!** In these forgiveness letters, you will directly and specifically address a person, project, experience, or situation that has failed you, hurt you or caused you pain in any way. For example, if you put your heart and soul into a project and it did not turn out the way you thought it would or produce the results you anticipated, that would be the perfect instance for a forgiveness letter. Perhaps you might even need to write yourself a letter, because of poor choices you made in the past. Describe each offense in separate, individual letters. Be specific. Pour your heart. Say whatever you need to say. This is a safe place. But here is the crucial key. In these letters, you will also *forgive* the persons, situations, experiences, or whatever your particular case might call for. You will completely and totally release them from the burden and responsibility of hurting you, letting you down, or not meeting your expectations. This is total absolution. As you release them, you will become free yourself. You will see who you are more clearly. Your self-perception will be clearer, and you will be freer to be yourself without the barriers (or crutches) of being angry at this person, frustrated by that experience, or labeled by this failure.

Take your time with this stage. Write as many letters as you need to. Remember to keep them in a safe place and to destroy them if necessary. Rewrite a given letter if you have to. You may write to a person, place, thing, situation, or experience as often you need to. For example, if you write a letter but realize at a later date that you are still angry, hurt, ashamed or disappointed, write another letter. Admit that you thought you were over it. Forgive again. Release again. Walk away from the pain again. If you earnestly repeat the process and work through the stage, this strategy will work and produce results. Remember, at some point when you are ready, you will make the decision to walk away from the pain forever and move on. When that time comes, you will know it. The memory of the pain may linger, but its power and influence over you and your decisions will be broken. Forgiveness brings freedom.

Prayer

Lord,

As I deal with the areas of unforgiveness in my life, help me to remember the wonderful gift of forgiveness you have given me through Jesus Christ. May I extend to others and to myself this same unconditional love and release, so that I can move on and not be hindered by them any longer. May they no longer block my view of who I am and what You see in me.

In Jesus Name,

Amen

Affirmations:

Forgiveness brings freedom.
I deserve freedom, so I will embrace forgiveness.
The pity party stops TODAY!
No weapon formed against me shall prosper.

Stage 5

Stepping Out as the New You!

Stage 5—Stepping Out as the New You!

Now that we have broken down many barriers and can better see the worth and value in ourselves, we must determine how to apply this knowledge to our everyday lives. Before you move too fast, take time and realize that you must be honest with *you*! If you are not, then your relationships will not be based on the new you, no matter how impacting this book has been. Make a commitment to be real with you, even when it hurts. And, most likely, it will hurt. Here are some helpful ways to get you started. Remember that you must keep God first and rely not on your strength alone but on the power of the Holy Spirit.

- Accept who you are—***all of you!***

- ***Honor yourself no matter what (Revisit Stage 1)***

- Affirm yourself

- Trust yourself

- Be kind to yourself

- Never forget that you will always have issues to deal with

- Be committed to doing the self-work that has to be done, even when it is inconvenient and painful. ***You are worth the effort!!***

- Never, ever, operate in fear and/or deceit

- Know your purpose, motive and desired outcome for all your actions.

- Live by *Philippians 2:3, "Let nothing be done through strive, or vain glory, but in lowliness of heart let each esteem the other better than themselves."*

- Your spiritual, emotional and intellectual development is YOUR RESPONSIBILITY. Do not leave it for someone else to do.

Comparisons and Conditions

Many times we cannot make lasting changes because there are old tapes continually playing in our heads. We are constantly comparing ourselves to others and placing conditions on our worthiness of love. Commit this list to memory, and when you hear those old tapes trying to play in your mind and spirit replace them those thoughts with ones you have learned by the work you've done in the is book.

Ten "10" Comparisons and Conditions to Avoid

- You would be so pretty if you lost weight or changed your hair.

- You are just like your mother (or father, sister, grandmother, etc.)—*meant in a negative way.*

- You will never be anything! Just look at you!

- I need to have as much as other people have in order to be as good as they are.

- That would have been a great idea, speech, sermon, etc., if only I/you had done this…

- I like the hairstyle, but it doesn't suit you

- I can never do anything right

- It is ALL my fault, I should have known better. *(Very rarely is any situation ALL our fault).*

- There must be something wrong with me, or I wouldn't be in this position.

- I wish I could sing, talk, dress, dance, or look like him or her.

- I would be happier if I had more money, a boyfriend/girlfriend, more clothes, etc.

A Healthy Self-Theology

The last thing we will do in our quest for a healthy self-image and positive self-esteem is to adopt a new *Self Theology.* Your *Self Theology* is a bit more than just self-esteem. Self-esteem is the steam behind you, so to speak. It is what tells you that you deserve a happy, fulfilled life and it gives you the strength to go get it. However your *Self Theology* is the personal theology, divine revelation or dogma that you hold pertaining to yourself. It is not based solely on your knowledge of you, but also on what God says about you. Your self esteem will push your *Self Theology* forward and create your life based upon the beliefs held in your *Self Theology.* Many of us were taught incorrect information about ourselves; and, unfortunately, that information became our *Self Theology.*

Let's adopt a new *Self Theology* and when those old tapes and negative thoughts try to invade our minds, we'll have something new to fight them with.

A Healthy Self-Theology

God loves me, I mean a lot to Him.
God honors me, I am His child.
God values me, He died for me.
God recognizes my worth, He orchestrated some things just for me.
God takes care of me, He delights in providing all my needs.
God planned for me, He chose me before the foundation of the world.
I am no accident, God meant for me to be saved and He even picked the day it would happen.
God delights in me and I bring Him joy, I am accepted in the beloved of His family.
When I reject myself, I am rejecting God's gift.

ABOUT THE AUTHOR

Veda McCoy is a graduate student at Wesley Theological Seminary in Washington, DC. She graduated with honors from Bowie State University in Bowie, MD with a degree in English. She has been in the ministry for over 20 years, including time spent as a national recording artist. She appeared along side Pastor Shirley Caesar on her live recording and video *"A Miracle in Harlem."*, in addition to releasing three of her own solo projects. Co-Pastor McCoy also traveled for many years as itinerary evangelist and workshop presenter. She has established several ministries targeted at meeting the needs of those who are broken, confused, and in need of direction. She has a peculiar gift for ministering to women in the Body of Christ. Co-Pastor McCoy has worked many years organizing and sponsoring conferences, workshops and fellowships. She is also an ordained elder in the Mt. Calvary Holy Churches of America, Inc., and continues to travel extensively as an itinerant preacher and workshop facilitator. In addition to these, Mrs. McCoy is a mentor, counselor and advisor. In 2004, she and her husband, Elder Marvin E. McCoy, founded Judah Christian Center in Washington, DC and they pastor the work together. She resides in Bowie, Maryland with her husband and two children.

Look for Veda McCoy's Next Book

"Purpose, Passion and Praise"
Sermons from and for the Heart"

Scheduled to be released January 2007

978-0-595-40675-3
0-595-40675-0

CPSIA information can be obtained at www.ICGtesting.com
Printed in the USA
BVOW05s1839150614

356283BV00003B/197/P